Kwela
B·O·O·K·S

This book – a recreation,
reinvention of an era – is dedicated to:

Granny Mosemphila, niece of the Bahwaduba tribesmen,
my dad Reuben Mlindi Masilela,
my mother Se'nnyane, daughter-in-law of our Dlambili clan,
and to the children Tebogo, Kgomotso
and beautiful Nokuthula, she who is named after
one of those who lie buried on the slopes of the Magaliesberg.

Contents

The author Johnny Masilela, then a couple of months old, relaxes on the lap of Klein-fontein Farm School pupil Mapula Kgasi.

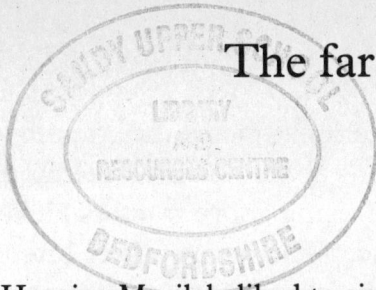

The farmhouse

Henrica Masilela liked to sing.

She was singing a lullaby on her way to the farmhouse, three weeks after the birth of her baby boy.

"Lamtietie, damtietie, slaap my kindjie," she sang, gently rocking the baby from side to side.

The footpath to the farmhouse twisted through the tobacco plants, over wooden bridges and across irrigational canals like one huge, long python.

For a period of three weeks Henrica and the baby had been indoors because in the African culture of the Transvaal, a baby may see light only after a certain period of time. In the case of Henrica's Ndebele in-laws, the set time was three weeks.

The third week for Henrica and the baby ended on a Monday morning, the day she was expected to take the baby to Venter, arguably the most successful tobacco farmer in Kleinfontein. The baby was being taken to the farmhouse at the request of farmer Venter himself. Like everyone else around Kleinfontein, Venter acknowledged and pitied Henrica for the suffering she went through before she could hold and cuddle a baby of her own.

"Lamtietie, damtietie, slaap my kindjie," sang Henrica with passion as she approached the farmhouse. How she prayed the little one would stop crying, or at least be quiet before she reached the farmhouse.

"Thula, precious one. Thula, we are about to enter the

important house of ol' Mr Venter and the mussus. Please be thula my child."

Her singing and the baby's cries attracted the attention of men and women at work on tobacco plants stretching endlessly towards a windmill rising above tractors kicking up red dust in the distance. The farmworkers lifted their faces from the dark green tobacco plants and rubbed their muddied hands against a barbed-wire fence separating the fields and the farmhouse.

Henrica and her baby looked immaculate in their new clothes, if one chose to compare their garments to the rags worn by those working in the tobacco fields. But such comparisons did not matter much to the farmworkers, for they all acknowledged that Henrica and her husband Reuben were educated and deserved better. Reuben Masilela was headmaster of Kleinfontein Farm School, where Henrica was the only other teacher.

Did the difference really matter? No, it didn't because the farmworkers had a deep understanding of the suffering the Masilelas had endured before they could cuddle and kiss a baby of their own. On seeing Henrica and the baby, they rose like one great storm. Waving at the mother and the baby, they removed the pieces of cloth protecting their mouths and noses from dust, revealing cheerful, smiling faces partly dirtied by the red soil.

After Henrica had waved back and passed on, the farmworkers started whispering among themselves about the rare occasion whereby one of them – with her baby – was to be allowed into the respected house of the Venters.

The farmhouse stood against the backdrop of a beautiful garden, and was painted white with maroon door panels, window frames and roof. There was no one on the brick and wiremesh front stoep, so Henrica walked a-round the house towards the back door.

"Lamtietie, damtietie. Slaap my kindjie."

There were two doors at the back entrance to the farm-house, a wiremesh one outside, and another further inside made of timber with a steel handle. On reaching the house, Henrica held the baby in one arm and, with much care, pulled at the door made of wiremesh and knocked gently on the inside panel. The handle was turned, gently, from the inside. Then the door was opened, slowly and carefully.

It was Johanna, the black woman who did the washing and cleaning for the Venters. Johanna gasped and clutched at her apron.

"Baas! It is Henrica and the baby!" she exclaimed, rush-ing back into the house.

A white man emerged from a front room, flashing tobacco-stained teeth. Venter was dressed in khaki shorts, a matching khaki shirt, a hat decorated with a leopard-hide band and velskoene. A camera hung by a strap around his neck.

"Ag siestog. What a pragtige little baby," said the beard-ed farmer. He stretched out two huge hairy arms, taking the baby from its mother.

It was a cute bundle of joy, with smooth cheeks, alert brown eyes, woolly, shiny black hair, and a cleft chin.

"Magtig. This cleft in the chin reminds me of the ou-baas my father," said Venter, chucking at the baby's chin. "Just like my father who died a long time ago." The white man then signalled for Henrica and Johanna to follow him into the front room.

For Henrica it was like walking on egg shells. The liv-ing room was beautiful. A table and chairs with feet carv-ed like the paws of a wild cat. Pictures of generations of white people on the walls next to a rifle and the heads of wild animals mounted on wooden bases.

"My magtig. Such a pragtige little thing," repeated farmer Venter, addressing his bespectacled wife who was running her hand through the red hair of a little boy with freckles who stood clutching at her floral dress. Little Peet, like his mother, looked at his father and the baby with much curiosity.

"Wie is die baba, Ma?" asked the little boy.

"Vra jou Pa," snapped the white woman.

At this point Henrica and Johanna nervously entered the front room, both stealing glances at Mrs Venter.

"Môre, missus Venter," greeted Henrica.

"Ja, Henrica," replied the bespectacled woman, curtly.

Venter himself threw a quick glance at his wife, then chucked the baby under the chin and handed him back to Henrica. He pulled out a pipe from his sock, used his free hand to check the pockets of his shorts and finally found a box of matches with which he lit the pipe. Mrs Venter's deep blue eyes followed her husband's every move. The boy Peet, seemingly confused by all this, also stared at his father.

"Nou ja, Henrica. I have been thinking." As if to demonstrate the seriousness of his thoughts, the man drew a lungful of smoke from the pipe. "As I was saying, Henrica. I have been thinking about a name for the baby." He paused for a moment, again inhaling a lungful of smoke. "This cleft on the chin. He's just like my own father, the oubaas. Now let me think about it. Ah, his name shall be Johannes. Johannes Gawie Venter, that was my father. Like your little Johannes here, my father had this cleft chin. How is the name, Henrica?"

"I think it is a good name, baas," replied Henrica, not really liking white people wanting to name other people's children.

"Baas? No Henrica. I have said to your husband, and I am saying it to you, I am not baas to you. To Johanna and the others, yes. But you and your husband, no. You just call me meneer. That should be fine."

"But what will the other white people think?" asked Henrica, stealing another glance at Mrs Venter.

"Do not worry yourself about the other white people," said Venter. "I am an important person in these parts. I built the school for the Bantu children when everyone else felt they did not need education. Jislaaik! It was my house that hosted Strijdom when he came to visit. No, do not tell me about the other whites. Call them baas if you like. Not me. Meneer is fine with me."

"If I may just come in there!" That was Mrs Venter. "Leon, you are becoming an embarrassment in this neighbourhood. You, Leon Stephanus Venter, are saying to a black woman not to worry about the dignity of the Boere of Kleinfontein. You are going to regret these statements one day!"

The white woman stormed from the scene, through a door into an adjacent room. And wept.

Venter's ears could pick up the choking sobs from the bedroom as well as Henrica's and Johanna's could. The two women did not say anything. It was Venter who chose to speak.

"Now I want you to follow me to the garden," he said. "A photograph on the tuinbank will certainly bring back memories of the old man, the oubaas." It was the first time that Henrica had gone through the front door of the farmhouse. Venter opened the door to the brick and wiremesh front stoep, and then another door into the front garden.

In the garden Venter ordered that Henrica, holding the baby in her arms, sit on a bench freshly painted red, green and yellow. Henrica sat down nervously on the bench, the one that was reputed to have served no less than three generations of Venters.

The man in khaki pressed his thumb into the pipe, and stuck the pipe back into his sock. He then moved backwards and planted one knee on the hard ground, with his camera at the ready. Venter flashed his tobacco-stained teeth in a smile. The baby did not respond as cheerfully as the man would have liked.

"Give us a smile. You are now seated where the oubaas sat daily before he died." Instead the baby looked up at its mother with a serious expression.

"Lamtietie, damtietie, give us a smile," sang Henrica softly, touching the baby's chin. There was a sudden spark in the baby's eyes. Venter was overwhelmed. "Turn him this way! Eyes to the camera! Pragtig!"

Click! the camera caught the cheerful smile and the cleft chin.

"Pragtig! Pragtig!" The farmworkers, who had tip-toed to the barbed-wire fence, rose and chanted in unison, their voices almost drowning the chug-chug of tractor engines in the distance.

"Pragtig," muttered Venter, tears blurring his sight and a lump in his throat. For, like the farmworkers he employed, the farmer had observed the previous year that the seventh of Henrica's babies had died at birth. Seven babies, and none of them had lived to the age of three weeks.

The headmaster

Kleinfontein Farm School was a small ash-brick building standing like a huge tomb against the backdrop of the Magaliesberg mountains. Aloe upon tall aloe rose from the cracked rock face, like spider legs about to pounce on the giggling barefooted children playing in the school grounds.

Attached to one end of the L-shaped structure was a little room with lots of books in it. 'Principal/Hoof' read a sign pinned askew to the door. Sitting behind a timber desk in the small office on that windy Monday morning was the headmaster, Reuben Masilela. A little orange-white-blue 'Republiek' flag flapped in the wind blowing through the half-closed door.

With darting brown eyes, the man with a long face was studying a white envelope over the rim of his thick-lensed spectacles. The envelope, with his name on it, had been the only letter to come out of the post office canvas bag. Not that too many letters dropped from the canvas bag, known as the 'privaatsak'.

Masilela turned the letter around in his hands. He pushed his glasses up the bridge of his nose with his finger and studied the address. He knew from the skewed handwriting that the letter came from Mosempila Kgosana, his mother-in-law, who lived in the town of Warmbaths in the Northern Transvaal. He tore open the flap and started reading quietly.

11

Dear son-in-law,

My heart was overcome with joy when I heard about the birth of the little one. To Henrica I say praise be unto the Good Lord, for according to the Book of Psalms, "He that goeth forth and weepeth, bearing precious seed, shall doubtless come again with rejoicing ..." As for you, my son, the Holy Bible has again been proven right, when it says "thy wife shall be as a fruitful vine by the sides of thine house, thy children like olive plants round about thy table." I cannot come soon because the white people who pay the pensions did not turn up. You, Reuben and Henrica, say in your letter the name of the child is Johannes. And you say the name came from the white man. Well, the two of you have adopted the ways of the white man. Tell me if you have not? Tell me because, like the white man, you drink tea with milk in it, in mugs made of polished bone. Johannes? But did I not say in my last letter that the child be named after his grandfather, Makhohlo, my own husband? Says the Book of Psalms: "Yea, thou shalt see thy children's children and peace upon Israel." The old man died before this special one was born. Ah, I must stop. I am crying again ...

Ding! dong! ding! dong! Masilela's gaze turned from the letter to the window, then through to the the boy chiming the school bell. Dressed in faded black shorts, with his oversized shirt flapping in the wind, July Maredi the bell-ringer struck at a piece of rail track hanging from a thorn tree branch.

Again July lifted the smaller iron bar in his hand and

12

struck at the school bell with the rhythm of one who had learnt his craft over time.

Ding! dong! ding! dong! For a third time the boy struck at the school bell, signalling the beginning of yet another school day.

A tall man, lean but strong, Masilela stood up and walked with long strides to the door. His small brown eyes darting behind his glasses, he surveyed the boy July from the doorway, and then the few who had gathered at the assembly point. The children knew and feared that look: the look of someone impatient and irritable with everything around him. For the third time Masilela dipped his hand into the little pocket of his waistcoat, pulled out a silver-plated Zobo, flipped open the top cover and checked the time.

Schoolchildren were now arriving in greater numbers at the assembly point opposite the headmaster's office, arranging themselves into rows according to the classroom they belonged to. Many were still running along footpaths from neighbouring farms, to beat what was known as the Last Bell. A few others were jumping from the backs of Bedford lorries driven by bearded white men in khaki, and the odd black truck driver in overalls.

The headmaster again glanced at his pocket-watch, growled, and peered over the rim of his glasses at July Maredi the bell-ringer. Although he never admitted it openly, Masilela liked July, who was the son of his good friend, old man Petrus Maredi.

"Stop!" ordered the headmaster. The bell-ringer stopped at once, and stood to attention as he had been taught. One minute, two minutes, three, four, five. "Now for the Last Bell!"

Ding! dong! ding! dong! The latecomers stopped dead in their tracks.

A girl stood with one foot glued to the ground and the other suspended in the air. An older boy screeched on his brakes, jumped off his bicycle and held it by his side. A handful of others stood still along pathways winding through tobacco fields, waiting for the worst to come.

When the sound of the Last Bell faded, the headmaster, growling all the time, retreated into his office and grabbed a cane lying on top of a filing cabinet.

"Broekskeur! broekskeur!" he snapped, re-emerging from his office with the stride of one in a great hurry to reach his destination. Then he suddenly stopped and his small brown eyes swept over the terrified faces of those who dared fail to beat the Last Bell. He strode to the front of the rows lined up at the assembly point, and looked at them for a while.

"All those who didn't come to Sunday school yesterday, to the right!" A shuffling of feet and dead silence.

The small brown eyes studied those left in rows. A growl. Fear and silence.

"Those who arrived late for Sunday school, also to the right!" Shuffling. Fear. Dead silence.

The lone figure of July Maredi stood by the school bell.

"And you!" snapped the headmaster throwing a fiery glance at the boy in the oversized shirt.

"Me, Sir? I came early, Sir. I came to ring the Sunday-school bell, Sir," replied July. Protesting. Pleading.

The headmaster gave another fierce glare at the latecomers. He turned to look at those who did not attend Sunday school. Then, using his free hand to hold the thin

14

end of the cane, he bent the stick this way and that way. Swish. "Broekskeur!"

Something caught his ear. His heart rose. And to the brief relief of all, a smile flashed across the long face.

"Lamtietie, damtietie. Slaap my kindjie," his wife sang as she walked down the foothpath leading from the headmaster's so-called Big House, pushing the baby in a pram.

Lighting up, the small brown eyes took a slow sweep across the faces, some of which had turned a smoky grey with terror. Then back to the mother and the baby. And back to those grey faces.

"Now move it! All to the assembly point at once!"

There were sighs of relief all round, as everyone dashed for the assembly area.

Henrica pushed the pram into the shade of the thorn tree where the bell-ringer stood to attention, and walked to the front. She stood next to her husband, cleared her throat and led the children in what had become the traditional first song at assembly:

... Father we thank Thee for the ni-i-ight
... one, two, three, four!

Kleinfontein Farm School headmaster Reuben Masilela, with his sister Sarah, pose in front of the Chevrolet at their father's farm in Winterveldt. Note Mr Masilela's "upmarket" outlook, complete in pyjamas and a gown.

The oil lamp

The headmaster's house was called the Big House by both farmworkers and schoolchildren. Despite the name, it was not a big house but a humble four-roomed dwelling built of ash-brick, standing between the main road to Thabazimbi and Kleinfontein Farm School. The Big House had, on one side, a garage for the headmaster's Chevrolet, and a flower garden in the front for his wife.

For a full three hours after the end of the school day, headmaster Reuben Masilela sat slumped in one of a set of sofas, staring blankly at the gramophone on top of a display cabinet. The stylish display cabinet, bought second-hand at Kleinfontein Farmers' Service, held many glasses and a cutlery set in neat rows behind the shining glass front. To the average farmworker in those parts a big house could not be better equipped.

Reuben Masilela hauled himself up, pulled out his Zobo and checked the time. It was ten minutes after the hour of three. He strode towards the gramophone, and played the title song from the original soundtrack of 'The sound of music'. It was a song he loved very much, and a song that lifted his spirits. When played softly, the motion picture soundtrack put him in the right mood to do lots of thinking. This time he was thinking about the little progress the newly established school had made.

How he wished he could extend the learning period to just before dusk. But he knew he couldn't. The farmers would be upset. Venter had built the school, on condition that at midday the farmers came in their Bedfords to pick up the little ones to work in the tobacco fields. But the fact that Venter had built the school in the first place was cause for celebration.

There was a brief soft moan from the cot next to the sofa, in which the baby slept peacefully.

Special indeed was the child Johannes. So special that many of the Kleinfontein farming community and their black employees came from near and far to see the baby. They came to express their joy towards headmaster Reuben and his wife, for the little gift with which the Good Lord had blessed them. They came because they had seen over time with tears in their eyes and lumps in their throats, that whenever Henrica gave birth, something would go wrong.

Masilela went to the window overlooking the Magaliesberg mountains, stretching majestically above the main road to Thabazimbi. He lifted his eyes to the beautiful view of the dark mountainside, where aloes rose from the cracked rock face. And the tallest of them all, against the slope and by the matted grass, was where all seven of his other babies were buried. The ones who never reached the age of three weeks.

Henrica's soprano flowed from the kitchen, blending beautifully with the melody from the gramophone.

… the hills are ali-i-ive, with the sound of mu-u-usic with songs they have su-u-ung, for a thousand yea-a-ars …

Still deep in thought, Masilela moved away from the window to the cot in which little Johannes was sleeping. He rocked the cot to and fro. Gently, gently indeed.

18

… the hills fill my hea-a-art, with the sound of
mu-u-usic …
my heart wants to beat like the wings of a bird …

"Henrica, my wife," Masilela called out, keeping his voice
as low as possible. "Will you come this way?"

Henrica emerged from the kitchen and stood in the doorway between the kitchen and living room, wiping her hands
with her apron. She was quick to notice her husband was
not in a happy mood.

"What's wrong now, Reuben?" she asked.

"It is this letter from Ma," he said. "Here it is."

Henrica took the single sheet of paper from the envelope and started reading silently. When she had finished
reading, she looked up at him and asked, "What are we
going to do?"

"I think we must send her money," he replied.

"But you know how's Ma. She will not accept it."

"Well, maybe we should consider that," replied Masilela.

"I must finish the cooking," Henrica said, stepping back
into the kitchen.

"Wait a minute." She stopped and looked at him.

"I am worried about the future of Johannes. We can't
bring up a decent child in an environment like Kleinfontein. Where else have you seen a people without a place
of worship?" He paused briefly. "I was very angry with
the children. Do you think their parents stop them from
attending Sunday school?" he asked, peering at his wife
over the rims of his spectacles.

"As I told you last night," said Henrica, "half of them
failed to attend. And the other half, they only came towards the end of the service."

"And the boy July Maredi. He tells me he did come on time."

Henrica was silent. Then she said, after a sigh, "I do not know. But I am afraid they seem to attend because they fear the cane."

"So the cane is working," he muttered, pulling the Zobo from his waistcoat. "I am not as fortunate with their parents. Good gracious! Something must be done about these people. July's father, old man Petrus Maredi, seems to understand. I must see him again tonight, about the others."

"I do not know. Try him. The problem with the people here ..."

"Is that they are not interested in a church!" he interrupted her. Masilela turned towards the window, the dark mountainside. And, as if addressing the aloes: "I, no the two of us, Henrica, have a moral obligation to bring them together and start a church. We owe it to the Good Lord. You continue with the Sunday school. The cane option will have to be considered from time to time, unfortunately." He straightened up and continued, "It's getting dark. I must see old man Maredi about the church. We really can't bring up our boy in such an environment."

He went for his hat and briefcase, closed the door behind him and strode down a footpath through the tobacco fields.

It was already dark when Masilela reached the door of Maredi's mud hut. Pushing his spectacles up the bridge of the nose, he knocked.

"Come in," answered the old man.

Masilela pushed the creaking door open, and entered the dark hut. A frail hand struck a match, lighting an oil

20

lamp made of a piece of string and a bottle of vaseline. There was a faint light, followed by a cloud of black smoke, and a stinging sensation in Masilela's eyes. The flame threatened to go out from the draught coming through a crack in the door.

"Ah, headmaster. It is good to see you. Sit down," said the old man, dressed in dusty blue overalls. His skin was wrinkled and his hair grey. He lifted a skinny hand, scratched his head, and then studied his dirty fingernails.

Masilela pulled a creaking chair away from a small table, placed his briefcase on the floor beside it and sat down.

"Thank you, friend," he muttered.

Old man Maredi chose the other chair and sat opposite the headmaster across the small table. A sigh. "So you are back."

"I'm back, friend. Back and troubled. God Almighty I'm troubled about Johannes, and all the black children of Kleinfontein."

"The children? What about the woman? The one who works at the farmhouse?"

"The woman Johanna? She says she cannot join the church. Sunday, she says, is the only time she can be with the children. She is sorry, she says she cannot come to the church." The small brown eyes darted behind the thick lenses.

"And the young man? The one who drives the truck of Venter?"

Masilela tilted the spectacles down the bridge of his nose, and peered at the old man over the rims for a long, tense moment.

"That one! He says the church is a place for white people. And I say to him, young man, the Good Lord loves you.

21

And he says the Lord loves white people! And you know what he says? He says the Lord loves white people and those who got educated at Kilnerton Teachers' College. That's me! That young fellow goes about telling the poor people the church is meant only for people like me!"

"Humble yourself, headmaster. You are getting heated up again. You do not understand these people. Leave them alone, I say. They will never ..."

"They must! Ah, humble myself." He pushed the spectacles up the bridge of his nose. "Yes, I must humble myself. But you must understand, friend. The white people have their own church. The stone church on the slopes of the Magaliesberg. We need to start our own church. And you say I must leave the farmworkers alone. People cannot go on like this, without a place of worship. Seriously, you must help me."

The old man sighed. His eyes dropped to the small table. He scratched his head, studied his fingernails and spoke with a heavy heart. "I do not understand, headmaster. Why don't you go to the stone church? You and Mrs Masilela are the learned ones among us. They will let you in."

"You know what it's like here. You are either white and a farmer, or black and a farmworker. But that's politics, you see. I'm not interested in politics. God Almighty lead us not into politics!" There followed a brief silence, before he continued. "My friend, we need a church for our people. And you must help me."

"Headmaster, I do not understand. I cannot read, I cannot write. How can I help you?" And he wiped sweat from his brow with the sleeve of his overalls.

"My friend, you are a humble old man. A man of God.

I want you to help me. God will provide you with the strength. And the wisdom."

A trickle of sweat ran down the old man's cheek, settling on his collar. "I do not understand. How can I help you, when I do not understand?"

Masilela opened his briefcase, and took out a dog-eared copy of the Holy Bible. "You need not know how to read and write to embrace the Lord". He flipped through the pages and read. Softly. "'For God so loved the world, that He gave His only begotten Son, that whoesoever believeth in Him should not perish, but have everlasting life.'" He peered at the old man. Neither said anything.

Then Maredi whispered, "Words of power. But frightening. It is like being led to the rope, by the hangman. I still do not understand. We are all going to die one day."

Masilela fixed his spectacles and turned his eyes back to the Bible spread on the small table. "'For God sent not His Son into the world, to condemn the world ...'"

"Please stop. Stop right there!" Maredi turned a little in the creaking chair, and called in the direction of a tattered curtain separating the small room from the dark part at the back. "Christina, my wife. Come this way. Come and listen to this."

There was a sigh and then slow, heavy footsteps from the dark. A huge big-eyed woman emerged from behind the curtain. Despite her size, Maredi's wife looked years younger than the old man. She slumped onto the floor, greeted the headmaster, patting one palm upon the other.

"Read on, teacher. Read to her as well. Maybe she will understand," said Maredi.

This time Masilela did not read from the Bible, but

spoke directly to Mrs Maredi. "I am talking to your husband about light and darkness. Darkness that men who do evil choose over light. I am visiting your house tonight to talk about this darkness, and the light."

Christina Maredi looked at her husband, and asked: "Do you understand, baba?"

Maredi did not understand, and indicated this by shaking his head. After much thought, Maredi's wife spoke again. "I remember when I was a child back home in Thabazimbi, my father belonged to a church. He wore colourful robes, and a headband made of strings of wool. But my father was sent back to Malawi before I could understand what his church was about ..."

His eyes lighting up, Masilela interrupted her. "Your father did find the light. The selfsame light I am talking about tonight. Now listen to this ... 'That light is come into the world, and men loved darkness rather than light, because their deeds were evil ... But he that doeth truth cometh to the light, that his deeds may be made manifest, that they are wrought in God.'"

The string in the lamp started to glow all by itself. Darkness was fast engulfing the place.

"Do we have more oil for the lamp, my wife?" asked Maredi.

"No, baba. There is no oil left in the house," she replied.

With a heavy heart, Masilela stood up and bid the two farewell, before adding, "Do not trouble yourselves with oil for the lamp, for one day ... one day everlasting light will enshrine your humble home!"

Maredi and his wife did not understand.

At the canal

The two boys stood on the banks of a canal that flowed through the tobacco farms of Kleinfontein. Peet Venter, the farmer's son, and Johannes Masilela, son of the farm-workers' school headmaster, stood with their short pants pulled down to their knees. They were each letting go with yellow urine that splashed into the canal.

Did it matter that downstream farmworkers scooped up the water in their palms and quenched the thirst of the hot days in the tobacco fields? Did it matter that some of the farmers themselves fished the occasional barbel out of the canal? Did it really matter?

"How far do you think the pee will go?" asked 12-year-old Peet, a red-haired boy with freckles. He was particularly enjoying that Saturday afternoon in the company of his younger black friend.

"We must go. My mommy is not going to like this," protested six-year-old Johannes, caressing a string of red and white beads around his neck. "And your mommy. You know how she scolds."

"Do not worry about my mommy and your mommy. They cannot find us here," Peet assured him. "Those beads, why do you wear them?"

"My mommy says it is family tradition. When some-one dies, the last child wears the beads. Me, I am the last of all the ones who died," said Johannes, pulling up his shorts. Suddenly he wagged a finger into the eyes of

Peet. "Hey, we must not talk about the ones who died. It makes my mommy cry."

Peet studied Johannes for a brief moment and nodded. "Yes, my ma also cries a lot about things."

"Things like what?" asked Johannes, hooking a finger into the string of beads.

"Like the farmworkers, you know," said Peet, still pointing his zol into the canal.

"Your mommy always scolds people." That was Johannes.

"Yes, Ma scolds, but only the farmworkers."

"You lying! You lying! Your mommy scolded my mommy the other day. My mommy does not work in the tobacco fields." Silence. Then again Johannes: "Why does your mommy scold at black people?"

"I do not know. Maybe because the black people don't want to work."

Johannes gathered some courage, then turned and looked his companion in the eye. "My mommy says your mommy does not like black people." Peet looked the other way. More silence. It made Johannes feel uneasy. "My daddy does not like Mommy to say such things, you know. He says the white people are kind to us."

Peet's face brightened. Just a flicker. "Does your mommy hate white people?"

"I do not know. But she says many things about white people."

"Like?"

"She says … she says white people go to another school. And black people go to another school."

"I do not know. But there are no black children at our school," replied Peet.

"And there are no white children at my daddy's school," added Johannes. Then, with a wink, he asked, "The Bedfords, do they pick up children at your school to work in the tobacco fields?"

"No," Peet smiled. "The children at our school are picked up by their mothers. Some go home on bicycles."

"The children at your school do not earn pocket money from the tobacco fields?"

"No, the children at our school get pocket money from their mothers," replied Peet. "Why?"

Johannes chose, instead, to ask his own question. "Does your mommy give you money?"

"No, she makes me home-made bread and soup. Sometimes she gives me candy floss."

"What is candy?"

"Candy floss is candy floss. It is like cotton wool."

Johannes caressed the string of beads and stared into the water. There was silence.

Then Peet, patting Johannes gently on the back, asked, "You know Tarzan?"

"Who?" asked Johannes, without interest.

"Tarzan. He's like the ape, he climbs from tree to tree. You don't know him?"

"Ape?" asked Johannes with a sparkle in his eye. "Does he work on the tobacco fields?"

"No, man, Tarzan works for nobody. He is a man of the jungle. Tarzan climbs from tree to tree. He's like the ape, man. Don't you understand?"

"My mommy says your mommy calls people who work on tobacco fields apes."

Peet looked the other way. "And you know what my

ma says? She says your daddy and your mommy are 'wysneusig', they think they know too much."

"Hey! Don't say that about Daddy and Mommy!" He scooped up a handful of sand and threw it into Peet's face.

The freckled boy ducked his head to the side, but some of the sand landed in his red hair. Peet yelled and charged forward, smacking Johannes across the face. There was a huge splash and Johannes began to scream, flailing his arms as he was swept downstream by the current.

Confused, Peet hesitated for a while. The blacks can't swim, Ma says! He must rescue him. Quickly he undressed, ran downstream to where Johannes was screaming, and dragged him to safety.

His eyes bulging, Johannes crouched on all fours, water dripping from his mouth and nostrils. He stopped vomitting and started crying. Peet quickly put on his clothes and lifted the smaller boy, dripping with water and tears, on to his back.

Johannes was still crying when Peet staggered along the footpath and quietly dropped him at the gate to the Big House.

Kleinfontien Farm School headmaster Reuben Masilela conducts a choir of bare-footed pupils on the foregrounds of the school. The author's mother Henrica, the one who likes to sing, says the girdles were handmade by herself and Mr Masilela's sister, Betty.

Merry Christmas!

My heart is filled with joy, for you have finally seen the light. You say in your letter he'd rather come and stay with me in Warmbaths. I told you that place is not good for him. Where have you seen a people without a church? Why do the people there not take a leaf from the white people, who have the lovely stone church on the mountainside? You say in your letter you will bring him to Warmbaths. I say no. I am his granny and I must pay for the visit. You remember what I said in my last letter. I said the sewing machine is bringing in money. I have even opened a savings book with the General Post Office. The last time I went to the GPO the baas at the counter said my money had given birth to 'calves'. Something the baas calls rente or interest. That means I have enough money for the train ticket. But I shall not come on the all-station choo-choo-makhala from Beit Bridge. I shall board the first-stop must-come-back from Pietersburg. If I board the choo-choo makhala I will miss the SAS bus from Pretoria station to Kleinfontein. The must-come-back is faster. It does not stop at Codrington and Pienaarsrivier and Wonderboom.

The thought of him moving in with me here fills my eyes with tears, tears of joy. I should not be missing the point if I quoted from the Book of Colossians, which reads: "Children, obey your parents in all things. For this is well pleasing unto the Lord." Perhaps I should be looking at St Mark, who said: "And they brought young children to him, that he should touch them: and his disciples rebuked those that brought them. But when Jesus saw it, he was much displeased, and said unto them, suffer the little children to come unto me, and forbid them not. For of such is the kingdom of God. Verily I say unto you. Whosoever shall not receive the kingdom of God as a little child, he shall not enter therein ..."

Granny arrived in Kleinfontein a few days before the morning of Christmas Eve, when she and Johannes boarded the maroon and white bus of the 'SAS', the Suid Afrikaanse Spoorweë, to the train station in Pretoria.

Granny's spectacles, which had seen many years, were held together with pieces of wire. No, the spectacles did not really matter, for on the day of the trip Granny was dressed in the stylish blue wrap-around of her times, the 'jikisa'. Johannes was somewhat uneasy with the way the old woman had stuffed some of the heavy luggage into a sewn-up goat skin, which she had tied around her waist and carried on her back like a baby. A bag hung from one hand while she held a black umbrella in the other. Johannes struggled alongside her carrying two more bags.

Sitting at the window, Johannes watched with awe as the bus made its way past the farms of Schoeman and De Villiers and Van Staden and many other farms he did not know. Wide-eyed, he asked Granny, "Nkoko, why when the bus runs fast, the trees also begin moving all over the place?"

"It is the wonders of the One up there," replied Granny, who was busy knitting something.

Johannes tried to figure out what really made the trees move when the bus moved, and when it stopped, made them also stop moving. Did the One up there want it to be that way? That when the trees moved …

"Come! You have to help carry the bags," Granny spoke with urgency as the bus stopped next to many other SASs at what Johannes guessed was the Pretoria train station.

Dressed in a sky-blue sailor's suit, matching blue socks, a blue hat and black Jack-and-Jill-design shoes with a strap over the instep, Johannes looked cute standing next to Granny at the train station. Patiently they waited among the crowds for the all-station 'choo-choo makhala', on its way back to Pietersburg, through Warmbaths. When the train arrived, the white people were the first to board at the Europeans-only Pretoria 'A' station, while the blacks waited their turn at Pretoria 'B', further down the tracks.

Puff! puff! puff! the black locomotive snailed its way into Pretoria 'B', with children from the European carriages waving at Johannes and other black passengers.

Johannes was sorry he could not wave back, because of the crazy scramble for seats, the heavy baggage, Granny's panicky scoldings, and the occasional swipe from her umbrella.

The railman in the navy blue uniform blew the whistle and waved a green flag from the tail-end carriage. Puff! puff! puff! the locomotive hauled its human cargo northwards.

In the compartment that Granny and Johannes shared with a number of other travellers, the first person he noticed was a little girl with a radiant smile and dimples. She wore a pink dress with frills and a matching pink ribbon tied in her plaited hair. The girl was travelling with an old man who, to judge from his exclamations and warmth, was acquainted with Granny.

"And who is the little warrior?" asked the old man.

In the intricate manner of tradition, Granny explained, "His name is Johannes. Son to my second daughter Henrica, who was named after one of the great-grandmothers of our clan, the great Bakgatla."

"Yes, I remember your daughter Henrica, she who got married to the teacher," replied the old man. "And yes, now I remember. I was on the delegation of elders who received the herd of cattle to pay for her marriage. That was a long time ago."

All the time Johannes stole quick glances at the pretty one with dimples who, according to the old man, was named Vuyisile, the daughter of one of his sons who lived in a place they called Soweto. Vuyisile was spending the Christmas holidays with her grandpa at Warmbaths.

"Ah, look at that … It reminds me of the grazing lands when I was a young warrior myself, looking after my father's cattle," sighed the old man, staring dreamily through the Springbok logo on the train window at the stretch of grassland alongside the railway track. It was a beautiful sight, with thorn trees and meadow stretching endlessly towards rolling hills in the distance.

On leaving the Hammanskraal railway station, the 'choo-choo-makhala' was almost half empty. Those left in the compartment now had more space and started searching through their baggage for 'skaftin', the food that passengers carry on long trips.

The old man ran his hands through the pockets of his jacket, took out two oranges, and gave one to Vuyisile.

From one of her bags Granny pulled a deep dish wrapped in a neat white cloth. She removed the cloth. The dish contained cold sorghum porridge. Granny then pulled out a cooldrink bottle – the type known as 'family size' – containing sour milk. She emptied a portion of the milk onto the porridge.

Johannes could not believe his eyes when the old lady started mixing the food with one wrinkled bare hand, then licking her messy fingers! Blushing, he threw a quick glance at Vuyisile. She rolled her eyes, clearly amused.

His heart beating furiously against his breast, Johannes refused to eat when Granny asked him to join her. He yearned for the train journey to come to an end.

As the carriages entered Warmbaths station, Johannes stood at the window watching with wide eyes the scores of rural folk lining the platform to welcome loved ones arriving in the choo-choo-makhala. Many of them wore ill-fitting, brightly coloured spectacles and waved all kinds of paraphernalia to mark the Christmas season.

Something touched Johannes's shoulder. When he turned around, he found himself face to face with Vuyisile. He looked away, breathing heavily against the Springbok logo on the window.

"Look at their clothes. Aren't they funny?" asked Vuyisile, pointing at the crowd singing and dancing on the platform.

"Merry Christmas! Merry Christmas to you from the big cities!" they chanted and panted.

Before Johannes could say a word – his first word to Vuyisile! – the train came gradually to a halt, with Granny scolding at him to help carry the luggage and to follow her.

It was when they started moving along the crowded platform that Johannes noticed that the old man walked with a limp, a condition which appeared to have been worsened by hours of sitting in the compartment.

"Take this, my friend, it should help your tired leg," said Granny offering her umbrella to the old man.

The old man and Vuyisile boarded the same bus to the black location as Johannes and Granny. The bus was so packed that Johannes's desire to talk to Vuyisile came to naught.

"Merry Christmas, old man. Merry Christmas, young man. And Merry Christmas, you out there," the people were chanting throughout the short bus trip to the location.

When the bus reached the terminus where everybody alighted, Granny and the old man bid each other farewell.

"My friend," said the old man to Granny, "ours is not such a big location. I shall give my niece Vuyisile directions to your place, so that she can bring the umbrella, the latest by tomorrow." Johannes looked forward to the visit with great anticipation.

When they reached Granny's place, Johannes's ears continued to pick up the 'Merry Christmas' chants from every corner of the location.

At bedtime Granny ordered Johannes to go down on his knees next to her, and to say the Lord's Prayer after her.

"... Forever, and ever, Amen," Johannes recited after the old lady, at the end of the prayer.

Granny made Johannes a sleeping place on the floor by her bedside. But before they went to bed, Granny asked Johannes, "Do you need to relieve yourself at night?"

Johannes replied that when such a need arose, he would normally do it outside of the house.

"Outside of the house? So the boy from Kleinfontein is

not scared of the ghosts of Warmbaths, heh?" said Granny. Johannes was frightened, but did not say so. But before Granny blew out the lantern, his attention was drawn to an object underneath the bed – a white chamber pot.

When the light went out, he heard drunken voices chanting "Merry Christmas! Merry Christmas to you too who has just put out the light!" Was it the ghosts, or just merrymakers? He closed his eyes tightly and covered his ears with his hands.

At last Johannes fell into a heavy sleep, only to be awoken later by a burning sensation in the area of his bladder. It took him some time to remember where he was. All the while his insides burned like a hot iron. He had to relieve himself, soon. But what about the ghosts Granny spoke about? He cringed. Ah, the chamber pot, he remembered. Cautiously he crawled towards the pot, lifting it with much care not to wake up Granny and tiptoed to the sitting room adjacent to Granny's bedroom.

Ta … ta … ta-trrr. Much relieved Johannes nearly half-filled the container. He tip-toed back to Granny's bedroom, and returned the chamber pot. He nearly jumped out of his skin when suddenly Granny snapped, "You dare forget to empty that thing in the morning!"

Shortly after dawn Granny's loud voice once again rang in his ears. Christmas Day! he thought, oh Christmas Day, and the new clothes! With the speed of lightning, Johannes went for the pair of new trousers specially bought for him for today, the new shirt and … But before he could put on the shoes something else struck his mind. The chamber pot!

With Granny's scolding echoing in his ears, Johannes crawled on all fours – new clothes and all – towards the chamber pot and carefully pulled the thing from under the bed. With the chamber pot in both hands, he hurried through the front door and towards the front gate. He threw a quick look at Granny who had on her spectacles and a pinafore. She was sweeping the yard.

"Look at what is the time! A grown-up like you, staggering from the house with the calabash of shame in your lazy hands."

Johannes shuffled through the gate, bound for the bushveld across the street. A number of people were boozing and dancing up and down the street, all the time chanting "Merry Christmas". They ululated and whistled even louder when they saw the young visitor clutching the enamel-plated container.

Ignoring them, Johannes took a few more steps into the street but then oops! Here was a girl in a brand new white dress with frills and a matching white ribbon tied in her plaited hair! She was carrying Granny's umbrella in both hands.

Johannes froze. Then, in a panic of rage and embarrassment, he swung around and hurled the chamber pot in the direction of the front door. For a terrible moment the thing spun in the air, its contents swirling and missing the sweeping Granny by a broom's breadth. The chamber pot hit the front wall with a bang. White enamel chips flew in all directions.

The people in the street laughed and ululated and whistled.

Johannes broke into a run, bolted for the front door and disappeared into Granny's house. His whole Christmas Day at Granny's was spent indoors, wide-eyed at the bedroom window, blushing.

Happy New Year!

"Come! come! Is easy man. See?" screamed one of the group as I stood on the banks of the dam at the place where white people played golf. His fingers pressed against his nose and the other hand covering his naked front, the boy hurled his body into the air, like he was a lamb that just had a bellyful from its mother. Head first, he hit the muddy ripples with a splash and disappeared under the red water.

"Help! He is going to drown!" I screamed at the others who were swimming in all directions. I was standing undressed on the banks of the dam, but did not have the guts to jump in and swim with them. I had not tried swimming before. Not in water so red with mud. Back in Kleinfontein, Mama always warned me that children who swam in dirty water would get bilharzia.

Anxiously I examined the surface of the water, but still there was no sign of the one who had been swallowed by the red bowels of the dam. We had to save this boy from drowning, or there would be trouble from Granny and the people at the location!

"Come! Is easy man. You just go swim swim, like this." Another swam in my direction, kicking the water with a rhythm that made my mouth gape with envy.

Suddenly there was a burning sensation in my eyes. Someone must have splashed the muddy water in my face. A wet hand caught my ankle. I kicked out, my hand slipping, and fell on my back.

Then as I rubbed the water from my eyes, someone shouted, "MaBoer!"

There was a lot of hissing and panting from the direction of the dam, as everyone swam with frantic strokes towards the banks. "MaBoer! MaBoer!" they were all screaming, with terror in their voices.

I continued rubbing my eyes and, hazy-eyed, I saw one after another grab his clothes, tuck them under his arm and bolt in the direction of the bushveld bordering the beautiful place where the white people played golf.

"Jou bloody kalgat!" came a voice from behind me. A golf stick whizzed past my ears, landing with a splash in the water.

I turned around and saw a group of white men in the distance, wielding golf sticks. I grabbed my clothes and ran after the others who were screaming at me to move fast. Two more golf sticks hit the ground, raising the dust next to me. I had to make a run for it, or I was dead!

"Run, you houtkop, run! The maBoer will kill you!"

I ran across the mowed grass like a very fast hare.

"Hy's soos 'n springbok!" shouted one of the white men, as I caught up with the other boys.

With water and sweat dripping down our naked bodies, we regrouped on one of the many winding footpaths in the bushveld. After we had put our clothes back on, someone wanted to know what we'd be doing the whole of New Year's Day.

"De rubbish dump," suggested someone else. They all agreed the rubbish dump would be the ideal place. I was not sure whether to agree to go along with them or not.

One of the boys, the one who I thought had drowned,

looked at me with a frown. "You want to go home to Mama?"

Scared to be seen as a sissy, I said I would love to go to the rubbish dump with them.

At the huge heap of ash and foul-smelling things, we found a tipper truck driver struggling to reverse into position. Before he could see us, we hid behind a clump of bushes. I was told that the health people did not like boys scratching around the rubbish dump.

Again the driver reversed towards a heap of rubbish. He stopped the truck, and reversed once more. I could hear him changing gear as he sent the truck forward, then reversed, tipping out a load of smelly things. A cloud of white dust rose from the ash heap. Coughing badly, the driver jumped out of the cabin, taking a brief look at the pile he had just unloaded. He prepared to haul himself back into the cabin. But first he pressed his finger against one nostril and let go with green snot, the full blob of which landed on my bare foot. The other boys giggled at this. Shyly, I rubbed my foot on the soft ground, as the truck drove away and disappeared in a cloud of dust.

The boys, laughing loudly this time, hurried towards the rubbish heap. Freshly unloaded refuse had plenty of surprises, they taught me. Like the odd piece of coal and perhaps fresh food from the dustbins of white people.

They all seemed to love scratching around the rubbish dump during this particular time of the year. New Year's Day was, for many of the people in the black location, not a time to scavenge and fight over leftover food. Many had working relatives visiting from the big cities with plenty of food and money.

40

We scratched deeper into the heap of newly unloaded garbage. I dug my hand into the filth and felt something elastic between my fingers. I scooped the thing out from underneath the rubbish. A pair of funny things, soft as Mama's night dress. I studied the garment for a while, sniffed at it, wondering just what on earth it was, and then threw the thing away and continued scratching around. The other boys burst into laughter.

"You know the thing you just threw away? It's knickers worn by white women in the movies." I had heard Mama talk about movies sometimes but I had never been to a place like that. I pretended to be deaf.

My fingers now emerged from the garbage clutching an old sock, which I sniffed at and threw away. More laughter from the other boys.

Groping around more desperately, I got hold of a plastic bag, which contained something heavy. A feeling of awe made my heart beat faster.

I put my hand into the plastic bag, pulling out a figure of Mary, the mother of Jesus Christ. I hesitated for a while and put the figure back into the plastic bag. The boys gathered around me. None of them seemed to know anything about Jesus Christ and the Virgin Mother.

"Dey say de women who work in the kitchen of white people steal things and hide dem in de dustbins," said the one who had splashed water into my eyes back at the dam, "and many of de things are taken by de rubbish truck."

"Hey! Dey say de people who pick things at de rubbish dump steal things from de graves!" said the one I thought had drowned. Then, pointing at the figure of Mary in my hand, he continued, "Dey mean things like dis."

Suddenly there was the screeching of tyres, followed by a cloud of dust.

"You blerry grave thieves, raise your hands and stay where you are!" boomed a voice from the road. Dressed in the khaki uniform and matching cap of the municipal police was a Coloured man.

"Hey! It is Willem de cop! Willem de cop!" the boys shouted as they bolted in all directions.

My whole body froze, like I was about to sneeze.

"Hands up, I said!" Willem shouted in my direction. He had cold deep eyes, this Coloured giant.

I placed the plastic bag by my feet and raised my hands. The deep eyes refused to shift from me. Willem slowly leaned his bicycle against a tree trunk. He took a step towards me. A second step ... I grabbed the plastic bag and broke into a run.

Cursing, Willem ran back to his bicycle and gave chase. He blew the silver whistle hanging from around his neck. "Stop, or I shoot, blerry grave thief!"

This did not scare me. Municipal cops, I had learned from the other boys, carried no guns. I bolted down the road in the direction of the location, the hems of my trousers flapping in the dust.

Prrr! Stop! Prrr! These sounds gave much-needed power to my feet. Willem's fat legs could hardly pedal fast enough to keep up with me. I turned on to a foot-path.

On reaching the location, I ran down the main street, maintaining as fast a pace as I could. I turned into the next street, sending a group of boys at a game of dice scattering in all directions.

"Stop him! He stole de ting from de place of de dead!"

The shrieking whistle and barking dogs brought people streaming out of their houses to watch.

"Stop him! He was hiding de ting by de place of de rubbish! Stop! Or I shoot!" The people in the streets did not try to stop me. Instead, they just laughed, either at me or at Willem the cop.

Up this street, down that one, up the next alley, and then down the next street. I turned into yet another side street and in my haste stepped into a muddy puddle and slipped, falling to the muddy ground.

The sound of bicycle tyres rang in my ears as I rubbed mud from my eyes.

Willem, panting and cursing, threw his bicycle to the ground and went for me. Flailing his hands in a desperate attempt to claw at my shirt collar, Willem's body suddenly started jerking, his teeth biting his tongue. Trembling from shock, I saw his hands freeze in mid-air. He squirmed. Foamy saliva ran from his mouth and he fell down like a huge bag of mielies.

I knew by the rolling of his red eyes, he had the sickness of people who faint from too much heat.

Kleinfontein Farm School headmaster Reuben Masilela stands behind three members of the staff and one of the many trophies he won during interschool eisteddfods. The picture was taken in 1968.

Letter to Raisibe

Uncle Jeremiah was a born-again Christian who rented a room adjacent to Granny's house. Very early one Sunday morning Granny arranged that I accompany Uncle Jeremiah to church.

I was waiting outside his room when Uncle Jeremiah emerged, dressed in oversized khaki trousers and clutching a copy of the Holy Bible under his arm. Uncle Jeremiah had a pair of small brown eyes which reminded me of a lamb's. "We have to go," he mumbled, leading the way.

The 'born-agains' had a tent put up on an unused piece of land on the outskirts of the location. We arrived at the tent to find other people seated on rows of benches. In the tent we boys and girls were required to sit in the front row. Just in front of us was the pastor who sat on a small chair behind a small table.

Unlike the hymns Daddy and Mama sang in Kleinfontein, the 'born-agains' sang their church songs loudly, clapping their hands all the time.

The pastor raised his hand, ordering the people to stop the singing and clapping and hallelujahs. He looked at me with eyes full of pity, and said, "Brothers and sisters in Christ, I have a wonderful message for all of us today. This message can be found in the Books of St Luke and Matthew. Although Brother Jeremiah would have preferred the Word to have been read from the Book of St

Mark, I choose to read our message from the Book of St Luke. 'And they brought unto him infants, that he would touch them. But when the disciples saw it, they rebuked them. But Jesus called them unto him, and said: Suffer little children to come unto me, and forbid them not, for of such is the kingdom of God. Verily I say unto you, whosoever shall not receive the kingdom of God as a little child, shall in no way enter therein ...'"

The pastor closed Bible. "Now let all those who embrace Jesus raise their hands and say hallelujah."

All the people raised their hands and said "hallelujah". I did not know whether to raise my hand or not. What if the pastor somehow found out I raised my hand simply because everybody else had their hands up? I sat there with my sweating hands clasped to my knees. The pastor asked that those who had embraced Jesus drop their hands and stand up. "And I mean only those who had their hands up."

Should I raise my hand, stand up, do both, or just sit? Nervously I remained on my seat.

"Let all of us who have embraced Jesus of Nazareth, close our eyes and say after me: Our Father, which art in heaven ..." Raising his voice to the heavens above, the pastor embarked on a long prayer, asking the Lord to help the people of the earth to triumph over sin, and to drive the Devil from our hearts.

"Forgive the Lamb among us today, Almighty, for he knows not what he is doing, hallelujah! It is so shocking, Christ our Lord ... Shocking indeed that we have among us what should be an innocent child, but is instead a child who has chosen Lucifer above you. I shall end by repeating the wisdom of St Luke, 'Verily I say unto you, whosoever shall not receive the kingdom of God as a little child shall in no way enter therein ...'"

At the end of the service everybody, including me and Uncle Jeremiah, left for home. On the way, Uncle Jeremiah did not speak much. I was scared I would be in trouble with Granny should Uncle Jeremiah tell her what had happened.

Instead, when we reached home, Uncle Jeremiah mumbled that I should follow him to his room. Was he going to lash me before explaining to Granny what happened? His eyes misty and his voice hoarse, Uncle Jeremiah mumbled that there was something he wanted to talk to me about.

In his room Uncle Jeremiah ordered that I sit on a stool next to a small table. On the table was a pencil and the kind of pad people use for writing letters.

Uncle Jeremiah moved to the window and rested his arms on the sill. For a long time I sat there, looking past his shoulder at the broken fencing and the dusty street, all the time wondering what Uncle Jeremiah was up to. But Uncle Jeremiah did not talk. He just stood there, neither moving nor speaking. He did not respond when an elderly cyclist in the street raised his hat to greet him. Nor did he seem to notice the drunk woman with an unlit cigarette dangling from between her cracked lips. Twice the woman asked to borrow matches, and twice Uncle Jeremiah did not respond. I wondered if he heard when the drunken woman finally mumbled a swear word and stumbled on.

Through the open window came the smell of the steam locomotive's smoke. I heard the chug-chug and then the whistle, as the 'must-come-back' from Messina to Pretoria approached the level crossing.

"'Leven o'clock," mumbled Uncle Jeremiah, at the same

time as I myself was muttering "'leven o'clock" by heart. Every day of my visit to Granny's place the train from Messina puffed its way over the level crossing at 11 o'clock, on its way to Pretoria.

Slowly Uncle Jeremiah turned away from the window and looked at me. Eyes still misty. He lifted his gaze to a white coat and a top hat hanging on the wall. "You see this coat?" Uncle Jeremiah spoke at last. "It is our uniform at the Little Kariba, where I work as a kitchenboy." He did not say why he kept a top hat.

As if reading my thoughts, Uncle Jeremiah removed the top hat from its hook and placed it on his head. He turned to a cracked mirror on the opposite wall and briefly smiled at his blurred image.

He picked up the pencil from the small table, turned it around in his fingers, and took a close curious look at the point and the pink eraser.

Eyes still full of tears, Uncle Jeremiah turned to me and asked with a whisper, "You know how to write?"

Yes, I did know how to write.

"I want you to write a letter for me," Uncle Jeremiah continued. "You know Raisibe?"

I knew Aunt Raisibe, the one who worked at the grocery store down the street.

"Take this and write a letter to her."

I held the pencil in my hand, confused. "Write what?" I asked.

"Write that I greet her in the name of our Lord Jesus Christ". I scribbled 'Dear Aunt Raisibe', and that Uncle Jeremiah greeted her in the name of Jesus Christ.

"Write that I live in this room all by my own. And that I am very lonely." I continued writing.

"Write that I love her so much. That I do not have the courage to say so. Write that at first I wanted to lie to her that I am the one who is writing this letter ... that because I love her so much I do not want to lie to her ...

"Write that I have asked you to write this letter because I have never been to school ...

"Write that ..." Uncle Jeremiah's body started jerking violently. He was sobbing uncontrollably. In between sobs he tried to mumble things about Aunt Raisibe, but I could not make out a word.

With some effort, he managed to plead, "Take it to her. Take the letter to Raisibe before it breaks my heart."

I hesitated, then folded the page neatly, and broke into a run.

I found Aunt Raisibe sweeping the store's front yard. Panting, I gave her the letter. She stepped back, looking at the piece of paper with eyes resembling hot coal.

"It is your letter ..." I told her. "Uncle sent me to bring the letter ... He is waiting for the answer."

"You blerry swine!" she retorted, throwing the letter in my face. "You bring dis ting to me knowing I cannot read! You make a idiot uneducate of me! I kill you, hear me?" Blows from the broom rained on my head, and I bolted back home.

I want Granny

Our house is a Big House. It is built of ash-brick and has four rooms. Our house has a garage on one side. Daddy keeps the '48 Chev in the garage. There is a garden of flowers at the front. Mama loves flowers. There are sofas in the Big House and a glass cabinet where Mama keeps the shining spoons and plates and cups and things. Daddy keeps his big books on the top shelf of the glass cabinet. On top of the cabinet is a gramophone. Daddy plays records on the gramophone. When the records play, Mama sings with them.

Mama is beautiful. Today she has her head covered in a scarf. There are patterns of flowers on the headscarf.

Daddy likes playing Jim Reeves on the gramophone. He stands up from the sofa, pulls out the Zobo and looks at it. Daddy likes pulling out his Zobo and checking the time. Time is important to Daddy.

The people who work on the tobacco farms do not have Zobos. They know the time by the shape and size of the shade of the marula trees and aloes, and the chiming of the school bell.

Daddy looks at his watch, then strides to the gramophone. He plays Jim Reeves.

> Take my ha-a-and, precious Lo-o-ord ...
> Lead me ho-o-ome, let me stand ...
> I'm ti-i-ired, I'm we-e-eak, I'm wo-o-orn ...

Daddy goes to the window. He looks at the aloes and marula trees on the foot of the Magalies.

"Nkosi yam, o Nkosi yam," Daddy speaks, as if to the mountain.

Who knows, maybe Daddy is speaking to the neat rows of stones below the tall aloe. The tall aloe over there is the place where Daddy's and Mama's other children are buried. I do not know any of the other childen. Daddy's brother, Uncle Luki, tells me they all died before I was born. Sometimes I wonder why they did not wait until I was born. But Mama's sister, Aunt Anna, says it is better that they died before I was born. Thinking about them would make me cry. Mama used to cry a lot about the ones who died.

Daddy likes playing music and standing at the window looking at the tall aloe.

Through the sto-o-orm, through the ni-i-ight …
Lead me on to the li-i-ight …
Take my ha-a-and, precious Lo-o-ord,
lead me o-o-on …

When Daddy plays music on the gramophone, Mama sings along. But today Mama is in the kitchen. She is not singing with Jim Reeves. Daddy looks at his Zobo, then goes to stand at the door between the kitchen and the sitting room. From the sofa in which I am slumped I cannot see Mama. But from the look in Daddy's brown eyes I know they are staring at each other. I can almost feel Mama dropping her eyes to stare at her hands. For some time, since Mama bought the headscarf, Daddy and Mama have been quarrelling. Daddy said Mrs Venter

51

and the other farmer's wives were complaining about the headscarf. Daddy did not say why but I once heard Mama laughing and talking to herself about it.

"Ha! Ha! Ha! Mrs Venter and them say ek raak wit! Me trying to be white! Hands off my looks, white man! As for you, Reuben, divorce me if you like!"

I do not know what the word divorce means, but Mama says it with such force it makes my stomach rumble.

'De force', it sounds like.

Mama's been working hard on her looks these days. She's been working on how best to do her hair. And how best to put on her headscarf.

If Mama is in a singing mood, she does not sing 'Nader my God by U' or 'Die Stem' or Jim Reeves as Daddy would have preferred. She sings about Mississippi and New Orleans. A song she calls Basin Street something.

From the fire in Daddy's eyes I know they will soon be saying strong words to each other. Daddy's glasses slip down the bridge of his nose. He peers at Mama over the rims.

"So you insist on wearing the headscarf?"

Mama is silent. I imagine her still staring down at her hands.

"I said you insist on wearing the damn scarf!"

Mama is silent. I leave the sofa, hurriedly walk past Daddy, and stand next to Mama. Somehow my standing next to Mama will make him stop it.

"Henrica! I am damn well talking to you!"

"Should the Boers decide what I should wear and what I should not?"

"Don't bring politics into this! I say are you going to defy me and continue wearing that damn thing?"

"Defy the Boers, yes! But you, I am not sure."

"Henrica ..." Daddy seems to have difficulty breathing. He pulls out the Zobo, checks the time. Daddy swings around and storms out of the house and disappears.

Mama is stroking my hair.

"Mama," I say.

"Yes, boy."

"Mama. I want to go to Granny."

"One of these days I'll take you to Granny, so that you should not see what hell is happening here," she replies, tears trickling down her cheeks.

Mama looks beautiful with those tears, and the headscarf.

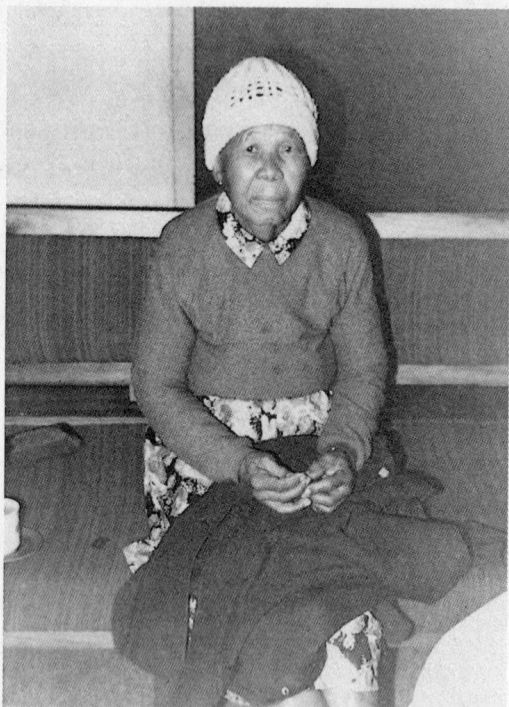

Granny Mosempila Kgosana, who was in the habit of always quoting from the Bible.

"Ons duck nie"

Mama has a little room in the sprawling Anglican church-yard at a place they call Lady Selborne, on the southern slopes of a mountain north of Pretoria.

There are so many people here that it is not possible to do the good things that Granny taught me. Granny taught me to help carry the baggage of the elderly. It did not matter even if they were strangers. But here there are so many people that even if one did not offer to help the elderly, one's Granny would never know. Everybody here seems not to care about everybody.

The other day I said my greetings to a drunken old lady, who responded by scolding me, saying I should mind my own business. "Son of a witch," she said, spitting at the ground near my feet. The people in the street laughed a lot at this, including even elderly men with rolled zols of tobacco between their lips.

All I could do was to fight back the tears, and not tell Mama about it. Mama was going through what she described as painful divorce with Dad, and I felt that moaning about the drunken woman would upset her even more.

Many of the people in Lady Selborne walk around with twisted faces, putting on a smiling mask whenever they meet important people like clergymen. The boys walk with their hands in their pockets, whistling. The girls stand at street corners and laugh so loudly that I swear it would make Daddy mad if he heard them.

Oh Daddy. I heard Mama say to Aunt Anna that Daddy was to marry another woman. I cannot imagine Daddy playing the gramophone for someone other than Mama singing in the kitchen. And Daddy, by now I can sing the lines from Jim Reeves, you know.

When my way grows drear ...
Precious Lo-o-ord linger nea-a-ar ...
When my li-i-ife's almost go-o-one ...
Hear my cry, hear my ca-a-all ...
Hold my ha-a-and lest I fa-a-all ...
Take my ha-a-and, precious Lo-o-ord,
lead me o-o-on ...

Granny fetched me from Kleinfontein to spend the Christmas holidays with her in Warmbaths. It was towards the end of the holidays that Mama came to pick me up from Warmbaths. She told Granny she wanted to show me her new place in Lady Selborne. So Mama moved from Kleinfontein?

Mama's new place is this little room in the churchyard, where she has all her belongings crammed together. A small bed. A Primus stove. A small table and chairs. A little FM radio, and piles of books on top of the small table. And headscarfs in many colours.

I have never seen a place like Lady Selborne before. It looks so grey, compared to the beauty of the farmsteads of Kleinfontein. The beautiful Magaliesberg mountains. The rock face and the aloes rising from there. Ah, and the tall aloe where Daddy and Mama's other children are buried.

"Mama," I say, "why do you have to live in this small room all by your own?"

"It's called freedom, boy!" Whatever that means.

Mama is also talking about the government which is to move the people of Lady Selborne to a place known as Mabopane, beyond the mountain. There Mama says she has registered her name for her own place. When the schools open, she will have moved there or at least she will travel by Putco bus until the government puts up a tent at her new place in Mabopane. A tent!

Mama says the government puts up tents to house people in Mabopane, and then it is up to the people to build houses of their own liking. Mama seems happy about this removal thing.

But the thing about moving from Lady Selborne makes the other people very angry. "Ons duck nie, ons phola hier," they sing, which I guess means they are refusing to move.

The schools are about to reopen, and Mama and Granny talk about taking me to a boarding school.

What? I feel like singing "ek duck nie, ek phola hier," but I do not have the courage.

I would have preferred to go to school in Warmbaths, but Granny says they do not have schools for higher learning there. All the children are sent to places like Pax College, or Setotoloane or Hwiti or Ratlhagana. Mama and Granny found a place for me at Ratlhagana High School.

The boarding house

We travelled by bus from Pienaarsrivier train station to Masobe, south of Warmbaths. Thorn trees and meadow border each side of the road to the village. The bush stretches beyond tall marula trees. And at the end of the road you can hear the chirping of the nsthare bird.

The villagers later told us if the ancestors are at peace with one's visit, one is welcomed by the moo of a cow.

No cow mooed, the villagers whispered to each other, when the bus transporting us drove its way through the village to the boarding house.

In the bus I sat next to a chubby but pretty little girl who openly wept at the thatched huts and goat trails and smell of cowdung. I pitied the way she was crying, and felt I should do something about it. I patted her on the shoulder and whispered, "Do not cry, plumpy. Soon you will get used to the place."

"I no plumpy! I is Suzy!" Tears were still trickling down her face as she spoke. There were giggles all round when I muttered, "I am sorry."

The bus swerved through the great gates of the boarding house, then turned left and brought it to a halt under a huge marula, standing between the boys' dormitories and the school building.

Perched on a hillside on the other side of Masobe was our boarding house, from which we were to walk every morning along winding footpaths to Ratlhagana High

School in the village. Most of the pupils were naughty boys and girls from the big cities who were taken to Masobe by their parents, with the hope of exposing them to the humble ways of the Bakgatla tribesmen.

Mama's and Granny's reasons for sending me here were not clear to me, but I think it had something to do with the troubles between Daddy and Mama in Kleinfontein.

One by one we jumped off the bus, boys and girls. One of the older boys climbed up a ladder at the back of the bus to throw our luggage down from the roof. There was a lot of whistling and singing from the dormitories. It made me feel uneasy. The air was hot, with a soft breeze rattling the tree's leaves with an eerie sound.

"This way, china!" A voice and a slap on the shoulder brought me back to my senses. "I say this way, china!"

I grabbed my bag and joined a group of terrified newcomers walking towards the dormitories. I managed a quick glance back and saw Suzy being herded by the older ones to the girls' dormitories on the other side of what looked like the teachers' quarters.

At Brixton dormitory, I lined up with the other newcomers and we were made to sing. There were many other humiliating things we were required to do, like the boy who was forced to telephone home using his shoe as the receiver, and the one who was forced to impersonate a Radio Bantu announcer inside a cardboard box.

It was at about midnight that the older boys became tired and went to sleep, leaving us to catch some sleep in the huge room reserved for newcomers.

The next morning all the boys got dressed in grey flannels and sky-blue shirts for the first day of the school year. The girls were dressed in grey gymslips and matching sky-blue shirts.

Proceedings at the morning assembly were led by an elderly, pipe-smoking headmaster who seemed to doze in his walk. The older boys called him Die Vader.

The girls stood in the front. I caught a glimpse of Suzy, beautiful in her grey gymnslip, still crying.

"And you, plump girl out there, whath wrong with you? Thith ith not the place for babies. You thut up!" warned a blushing young teacher with bushy brows. It was then I noticed the young teacher had no teeth. Suzy blurted out a brief choking sob, which made my heart bleed. I felt like walking up to the young teacher, punching him in the face and making his nose bleed.

Someone nudged me from behind. It was Pompie, the one who had herded us from the bus to the dormitories the previous day.

"She your baby?" Pompie whispered.

"Yes," I muttered.

"You lie. Who she?"

"Suzy," I replied.

"You lie."

I did not reply. Instead Die Vader removed his pipe from his mouth and started addressing us.

"Goo ... good, morning boys and ... and girls. Wel ... welcome to Ratlhagana High School. I wel ... welcome especially the new ones. Let me star ... start by introducing you to our ... to our new member of the staff, English teacher, Mr Masubelele. Give him a big hand." So Bushy Eyebrows and his lisping tongue was also new at the school!

We welcomed the new teacher with a round of applause.

From the assembly point we marched to our classrooms to the beat of kettledrums.

Suzy stopped crying when we filed into the Form One classroom. All the shuffling and giggling came to a dead stop when English teacher Bushy Eyebrows walked in carrying some books and a cane.

"Good morning boyth and girlth, my name, ath the head-mathter hath, already told you, ith Mr Mathubelele," he said blushing. He turned and walked to the window and stood there, scanning the main entrance to the premises.

To me Mr Masubelele looked too young to be a teacher and, moreover, why did he act so restless?

Someone struck the school bell suspended between two poles to signal a short break. We ran out to play, to relieve ourselves or, the older ones, to smoke behind the toilets.

I chose to stand under the shade of the marula, watching Suzy and the other girls chasing each other all over the place. Then I saw Pompie and two other older boys come running from the direction of the toilets. Pompie and his companions went straight to the girls, called Suzy aside and whispered something that made her blush and flail her hands in the air. All the time Pompie and the other boys were pointing at me, although I could not hear what they were saying.

Suzy broke from the group and confronted me. "You say I is your baby. You lie! You lie!" This was followed by laughter from all over the school grounds.

Blushing with a mixture of embarrassment and rage, I left the giggling group and dashed to the toilets.

There I undid my zip and let off a trickle of urine as the bell was ringing. The thought of Mr Masubelele and his cane made me run for dear life back to the classroom. But

I was too late. All the other pupils had already taken their places. Mr Masubelele ordered me to stand in front.

Suzy seemed to be embarrassed, or else pitied me, which made my heart beat faster.

"Ith thith the time to return to clath?" charged Mr Masubelele. "And hey, look at him, hith zip ith undone!"

For a moment the teacher swept his eyes over the giggling faces of the pupils. His gaze stopped at Suzy, who was not giggling like the others. She seemed to sympathise with me! "You there who pretend to be reading. I want you to come in front and fix hith zip."

Suzy hesitated, then walked to the front to fix my trousers. The other pupils were laughing loudly at all this. Mr Masubelele ordered Suzy and me to take our seats.

"You will obviouthly want to know a little more about me, won't you?"

"Yes sir," they all replied, except for me and my Suzy.

"Well, I come from … Thall I thay I am from …" There was the sound of a car engine at the main entrance which seemed to send a jolt up Mr Masubelele's spine. Those of us who sat next to the windows saw a cream Mercedes drive through the great gates and come to a halt under the marula tree.

Mr Masubelele threw one look at the car and started trembling, with sweat beads growing all over his face, like one who was falling ill. After a few moments, he walked hurriedly out of the classroom.

The story of Mr Masubelele's strange behaviour was explained later by the older boys at the dormitories. The occupants of the motor car who put the scare into Mr Masubelele were his parents, who had managed to track him down after a long search. Bushy Eyebrows was a university student who had played truant from his own studies, and conned Die Vader into employing him as the English teacher.

Aunt Betty who helped in weaving the girdles for the Kleinfontein Farm School girls. The picture was taken in 1960.

The dream of Mafikeng

The scent of ripe marula fruit reminded me of Klein-fontein, where marula trees dotted the mountainside. I was sitting under the shade of the marula in the boarding school yard, just as I used to sit two years earlier when I first came to Masobe.

I was sitting under the marula all by myself, observing Die Vader as he emerged from his room at the teachers' quarters. The headmaster had a crop of snow white hair perched atop his wrinkled, oval-shaped face, and fairly steady hands for one so old.

On that particular Sunday morning Die Vader looked even older and more weary. I knew what was troubling him, as did everyone else at the boarding house. Rumours about the men from Mafikeng and their dreams of a Tswana-speaking enclave were spreading fast. The future was becoming uncertain for Die Vader, being a descendant of the Amandebele-A-Moletlane in the Northern Transvaal, and equally uncertain for all others who were not of Setswana origin.

I had over the years developed a liking for Die Vader. His grandfatherly manner, the pipe and his religious passions. Just like Dad.

Looking at Die Vader now, I remembered when at the Friday morning assembly, with a lump in his throat, he addressed us: "Child ... children, oh my children. You mus ... must have heard about the school soon to ... be

taken over by other people. You ... you may be see ...
seeing me for the last time this year. I hear the ... the
Tswanas may replace me with one of their own. What
shall I do, oh child ... children my children, but pack
and head home where ... where I can ... can be buried
in peace, among my own."

From that day I had closely watched Die Vader's sad
face, when he walked through the school yard, for example, or worked with what looked like a blunt hoe in his
maize patch. I also remembered with guilt how we had
sometimes stolen mielie cobs and watermelons from the
old man's harvest.

On this particular Sunday, Die Vader was dressed in a
black cassock, carrying the brown leather briefcase in
which were the Holy Bible and the hymn book. I knew at
once he was on his way to the local Anglican Church
where the headmaster was a lay preacher. Again the frail
figure of Die Vader walking along the village pathways in
those church clothes brought back memories of my dad.
It also made me feel like finding those responsible for
this uncertainty and punching them on the nose.

When Die Vader disappeared along the path that wound
behind the thatched huts, I returned to the dormitory.
There I found the other boys sitting in a half-circle, listening to Pompie. He was lecturing them about Nkurumah
again, I thought to myself. Pompie, who came from Soweto, taught us a lot of things about the struggle of black
people against the wrath of white oppression. At first the
struggle sounded like the things Mama used to say about
Peet's mother, Mrs Venter, and the other white people of
Kleinfontein. The people of Soweto, perhaps among them
the pretty Vuyisile I had met in the train with Granny,
were at the forefront of the struggle.

"The tree of liberty," Pompie would charge, "will be watered by the blood of the martyrs." I joined the others listening to Pompie, because what he had been teaching us over the years made increasing sense.

"Dey say de white man is to give black people indepence," he was saying.

"You mean de underpants like we wear?" asked Jan Raboroko, the hunchback.

"No, man! Don't be silly! Indepence is white man cut pieces of land for de blacks. Dey say de village chiefs is become like Vorster, Prime Ministers."

"And why is Die Vader troubled?"

"He is troubled because dey say the Tswanas must teach their own. Die Vader is not Tswana."

"What is the chief say?"

"I know! I know!" chipped in Jan Raboboroko, scratching his hunchback. "Die Vader told me the chief also like this thing about the Tswanas. He say the chief wants someone Tswana to take over."

"What about all of us who are not Tswanas?" More and more boys started firing questions.

"I don't know," replied Pompie. "Maybe we will also be ordered to leave with Die Vader."

And when finally one of the boys asked, "What is to be done?" it was Pompie who replied. "In Soweto pupils like us are marching to protest against oppression. Maybe we should march on the chief."

I, like everyone else, liked the idea, and said so.

A committee of three, including me as the organiser, was chosen to work out the day and time on which we would march.

67

Marching on goat trails

"Mooo!" echoed one of the village cows on the return of Chief Maloka, when he was recalled from his employment as a gardener at Kilnerton College for trainee black teachers outside Pretoria.

It was on the day that the Bakgatla gathered at the tribal kgotla for the great feast to welcome Chief Maloka, that the inmates at the boarding house had their own meeting with their own agenda. There were stark differences between the gathering at the boarding house and the great feast to welcome Chief Maloka. While the boys at the boarding house were seething with rage, the villagers were excitedly looking forward to the great feast.

"Where do all the village pathways lead today, mender of the goat hides?" a young herdboy asked the elderly cobbler.

The cobbler replied, "Where else, young keeper of the Bakgatla stock, if not to the great feast of our chief?"

More and more tribesmen passed by on their way to the great feast. Like the crippled woman who was pushed to the place in a creaking wheelbarrow, and the hewer of wood who walked with a limp.

"Say, old man. Where are all these people bound for?" asked the one in the wheelbarrow of the limping hewer of wood.

"Where else mother, if not for the great feast to welcome the feared one?" replied the hewer of wood, limping on towards the kgotla.

Some years before, at Kilnerton College, Chief Maloka had made friends with a brilliant young teacher, Reuben Masilela, who wore spectacles with a thick black rim. Whenever upset with fellow students, the young fellow had the habit of tilting his spectacles down the bridge of his nose and peering at his fellows for a moment.

Now, before returning to Masobe, Chief Maloka had bought himself a pair of spectacles with thick black rims. On the day of the feast, he sat in the royal armchair draped in the hide of a leopard. From time to time he would tilt his spectacles down the bridge of his nose and peer at members of his tribe for a very long moment indeed.

Someone pounded the cowhide drum, triggering whistles and shrieks from the warriors and maidens.

Dikeledi, she with the backside that resembled the tail of a ram ... she with the breasts as smooth as the eggs of the ntshare, was the first to take to the dance floor. With the elegance of a wild goose, Dikeledi gyrated to the rhythm of the drum, dancing her way out from the rows of other maidens. She thrust her breasts outwards and then inwards, triggering shrieks and whistles from the villagers.

"What a beautiful woman!" the men gasped. But as they say, the beauty of a maiden is not measured by mere looks.

Overwhelmed by Dikeledi's reception, a young warrior emerged from among the male dancers, flexing his muscles to the delight of the villagers. Again he leapt forward, charging this way and that. When he leapt into the empty air, landing in the dust on one knee, the entire regiment of warriors threw themselves to the ground, and then rose like one great storm. The villagers greeted them with more whistles and ululating.

Chief Maloka raised his hand, ordering that the dancing must stop. He tilted his spectacles to the bridge of his nose. "I greet you, the proud Bakgatla. I greet you in the name of my father, his father and his father's father," Chief Maloka spoke, amidst whistling and ululating and the blowing of the bullhorn.

"I do not have much to tell you about this great gathering, for words of wisdom have been spoken by my father and his father before him. And the message, as you all know and your children should know, is that we the Bakgatla are a tribe that conducts itself with dignity at all times," Chief Maloka said.

He stopped for a while, and called out the traditional Bakgatla tribal slogan: "Peace unto the land and the cattle and the people of Masobe!"

"Peace unto our great chief!" they replied.

The ceremony was a joyful occasion. The Bakgatla were indeed happy to have their chief back.

Some days later an elderly headman from the riverside visited.

"I come to you, oh feared one. I come to bring news," the headman spoke with the urgency of someone who had little time on his side, and his troubled gaze kept wandering towards a cluster of bushes on the hillside.

Chief Maloka removed his spectacles, wiped the lenses, pushed the glasses up to his eyes and back down to the tip of his nose.

"Say, what news have you brought? You who went through mountain school with my own father. Say, is it about the flock of birds that have been feeding on the sprouting crops?"

"No, it is not about the birds, feared one ..."

"Say then, what is it? Is it about the rain clouds, the herdboys? Say, what do you mean, old man?"

"You tell the truth, feared one. I am an old man now. My hair is grey, my skin is wrinkled. I bring news to you feared one, news which you will not like."

"News which I will not like? Say old man, what is the news? Is it another visit from the ancestors? Say, what is it?"

"It is the boys at the boarding house, feared one. They gathered on the day of the great feast, saying things about the chieftainship. They ... I am afraid they are revolting against you, feared one."

"What! How can anyone revolt against the chieftainship, against me?"

"They say our chieftainship is the creation of white people, a creation of Apartheid," the old man continued.

"I do not understand," replied Chief Maloka nervously fingering his spectacles. "What says Lediga, what says our village churchman and what say the other men of the tribal council?"

"You must understand, feared one. Time is not on our side. Right now as I speak to you, the boys are about to descend on the kgotla like a swarm of locusts. Something they call a march."

And as the elderly headman was trying to explain further, his voice was drowned by hisses and chants from the direction of the hill: "Hoosh! hoosh! hai! hai!"

Hundreds of boys and girls were coming down the hill, kicking up choking dust from the goat and cattle trails. The smell of trampled cowdung filled the air. They converged on the royal enclave in dance and song, holding placards and demanding the resignation of Chief Maloka.

Chief Maloka sat on the edge of the seat of his arm-chair, staring at them in stunned silence. One placard caught his eye, the one that read 'Down With Tribalism!' Chief Maloka tilted the rim of his spectacles and peered at the youth holding the placard aloft. He was a light-skinned fellow with a cleft chin, and reminded the chief of someone he knew.

Chief Maloka whispered into the ear of the old man. The old man whispered back, "His name is Johannes, son to Reuben Masilela, the respected schoolmaster in Kleinfontein."

Henrica Masilela (seated left) shortly after she had moved to the Pretoria township of Lady Selborne. With her are family friend the late Totsi Dube (seated right), Henrica's younger sister Aunt Ann and her late husband Jeff Ntsele.

Deliver us from evil

Dear son-in-law,
I am hurting sore. The news of the break-up of your marriage with my daughter continues to pain me. I try to forget, but it is hard. The picture of the wedding on my bedroom wall is a painful reminder of how it all started. I still have the letter in which you broke the news of the birth of Johannes. A tear stains the place where you signed your name, all those many years ago. In the letter, you said Henrica sang and that the white man shed a tear. That was when the white man took his picture on the garden bench. There is a lump in my throat about the break-up of your marriage with Henrica. When I heard about it I swore to God never to talk to the two of you again.

Henrica was here. She says I need not worry. She says she is happy with her new teaching job at a place they call Mabopane, near Pretoria. That does not heal the hurt in me. From time to time I draw solace from the Book of St Mark: "Behold, there went out a sower to sow. And it came to pass, as he sowed, some fell by the wayside, and the fowls of the air came and devoured it up. And some fell on stony ground. And some fell among thorns, and the thorns grew up, and choked it, and yielded no fruit." Our father, who art in Heaven, I must not cry now.

When Johannes returned home, I could see something was very wrong. He refused to talk to me about it. But through the fellowship of God and the Holy Spirit, I met a mender of cattle and goat hides from the village of Masobe at the Bantu Commissioner's office. The old man told the truth of what had taken place at the village kgotla. The painful truth.

The mender of hides tells me the Bakgatla tribesmen called a great feast to celebrate the return of their leader Chief Maloka. Tribesmen from across the grassland of lovely Masobe were there to welcome the feared one. The mender of hides tells of the many who arrived, the herdboys and the man who carves wood and, above all, the village churchman who still wears a cassock with holes in it.

But unbeknown to the tribesmen, as they gathered at the kgotla, another meeting was taking place at the boarding house. A gathering the mender of goat hides says had evil intentions. A meeting which Johannes attended.

Then a few days after the great gathering of the Bakgatla and this other meeting (with evil intentions), a village elder visited the tribal chief, to say the boys and girls at the boarding house were to invade the kgotla. Masobe had seen nothing like it before. As the village elder was consulting with the chief, the boys and girls arrived, demanding that Chief Maloka relieve himself of his position at the head of the tribe. The boys accused Chief Maloka of working with the government to remove the headmaster from their school. In great numbers, the children descended on the kgotla, tearing to pieces the ancient dignity of the Bakgatla chieftainship. Chief

Maloka, the mender of the hides tells me, consulted briefly with the village elder, then collapsed and died.

A few days thereafter, two important men arrived at the boarding house. The men, one white and the other one of us, drove into the premises in a government vehicle. The driver was a white man with a neat red moustache, and the other, one of our people, was a big gentleman with a crop of woolly grey hair. He is a mmoki, this mender of cattle and goat hides – a man who makes words sing. He told me how they were dressed – in grey suits – and even how the black one spoke. As if the mender of hides was in the office where the boys were called in, one by one.

"Your name is Johannes Masilela, right?" The black was the first to speak to him. He then asked Johannes to say what happened at the kgotla. The boy mumbled, "There was a march." The man wanted to know who started it all. Johannes was silent. And, the mender of hides tells, the man got angry. He told Johannes the other boys had said he was the one who came with the idea of the march. God Almighty!

I do not know if these are the white man's exact words, but the mender of the hides swears they are. He said, "You are well aware, Johannes Masilela, that in terms of the rules of the Department of Bantu Education, you shall not incite other children into wrongdoing. I am not going to waste my time, and that of the assistant inspector, by reading rules that you should know by heart. You are a bad influence on other children. The headmaster will forthwith be instructed to give you a letter explaining to your parents what kind of example you are. And you shall be asked to pack your things and leave these premises, never to return."

And so he is here now. He is very silent. He will not talk. Poor old me. What must I do? Oh God of Abraham.

… Deliver us from evil.

Glossary of non-English words

ag siestog – expression indicating sympathy; oh shame

baas – reference by black workers to the white master

baba – baby (Afrikaans); father (isiZulu)

blerry – bloody

Boere – here, Afrikaans-speaking descendents of the citizens of the old Transvaal republic of President Paul Kruger

broekskeur! – expression used by school teachers, particularly those influenced by the Afrikaans language, threatening how they would flog a pupil until his pants split/tear

Die Stem – official South African national anthem until 1994, when it was combined with the Nguni version of Nkosi Sikelel 'iAfrika to become part of the new national anthem

Die Vader – literally 'The Father' – reference by pupils to their headmaster

(ek) raak wit – literally '(I) become white' – a black person being accused of behaving and 'becoming' like a white

houtkop – expression used by school teachers, again especially in areas influenced by the Afrikaans language, to describe someone whose brains were like a piece of wood

Hy's soos 'n springbok – He's like a springbok

jikisa – township slang for the wrap-around type of dress popular with elderly women

jislaaik – exclamation expressing surprise

Jou bloody kaalgat! – You bloody bare bum!

kgotla – a tribal chief's entire homestead, including the place where villagers gather for meetings

Lamtietie, damtietie, slaap my kindjie – lullaby borrowed from the Afrikaans language

MaBoer – in Setswana 'ma' means 'the', therefore 'maBoer' simply refers to 'the Boers'

magtig! – good gracious!

makhala – whistling of a locomotive

meneer – sir; Mr

mielie(s) – maize

mmoki – praise singer (Setswana)

môre – (good) morning

Nader my God by U – Afrikaans version of the hymn 'Nearer my God to Thee'

Nkoko – Grandmother

Nkosi yam! – My Lord!

Nou ja – Well …

Ons duck nie, ons phola hier – township slang battle-cry of the fifties and sixties when blacks under threat of forced removal vowed not to move an inch

oubaas – elderly/old master

pragtig(e) – wonderful; pretty; beautiful

privaatsak – in the old post-office system institutions like schools and churches had their own 'private bag' in which their mail was delivered to their door

rente – interest

Republiek – Republic (of South Africa)

SAS/Suid-Afrikaanse Spoorweë – old South African Railways

skaftin – township slang for food provisions carried by travellers

stoep – veranda

thula – be quiet

tuinbank – garden bench

velskoene – home-made leather shoes popular with Afrikaans-speaking farmers to this day

Vra jou pa – Ask your dad

Wie is die baba? – Who is the baby?

wysneusig – pedantic; used in this context to describe someone who thinks he/she knows everything

zol – cigarette made of loose tobacco or dagga rolled in strips of newspaper or brown paper; here also used as a metaphor for penis